GHOST STORIES

GHOSTS IN PRISONS

By Lisa Owings

EPIC

BELLWETHER MEDIA • MINNEAPOLIS, MN

EPIC BOOKS are no ordinary books. They burst with intense action, high-speed heroics, and shadows of the unknown. Are you ready for an Epic adventure?

This edition first published in 2017 by Bellwether Media, Inc.

No part of this publication may be reproduced in whole or in part without written permission of the publisher.
For information regarding permission, write to Bellwether Media, Inc., Attention: Permissions Department,
5357 Penn Avenue South, Minneapolis, MN 55419.

Library of Congress Cataloging-in-Publication Data

Names: Owings, Lisa, author.
Title: Ghosts in Prisons / by Lisa Owings.
Description: Minneapolis, MN : Bellwether Media Inc., 2017. | Series: Epic:
 Ghost Stories | Includes bibliographical references and index.
Identifiers: LCCN 2016001378 | ISBN 9781626174313 (hardcover : alk. paper)
Subjects: LCSH: Haunted prisons–United States–Juvenile literature. |
 Ghosts–United States–Juvenile literature.
Classification: LCC BF1477.3 .O95 2017 | DDC 133.1/22–dc23
LC record available at http://lccn.loc.gov/2016001378

Printed in the United States of America, North Mankato, MN.

TABLE OF CONTENTS

AFTERLIFE SENTENCE

Your evening prison tour just ended. You walk back past dark, empty cells.

Suddenly, a cold hand brushes the back of your neck. You turn. No one is behind you. Did you **disturb** a prisoner's ghost?

HAUNTED BY CRIMES

Al Capone was a Chicago **gangster**. He used crime to gain wealth and power.

Al Capone

newspaper headline text

THREE CENTS THE

54TH YEAR—39.

MASSA

HAFFA CHANGES HIS MIND; WILL FIGHT PRISON

TWO OF VICT

Owe... to Friends. He ...kes Bond. Pre- ... Appeal.

...N COUNCIL

...he county jail. ...43d ward, fre- ...s changed his ...e will fight ...al prison to ...ce for boot- ...ged yester- ... without a ...t batch of ...t for Leav- ...Today he ...ed States ...to bear

...after- ...Lindsey ...build- ...a se- ...affa's ...uths's

...STAYS GIVEN 2 ...F 3 KILLERS DUE ...TO DIE TONIGHT

...s Faces the Electric ...r Alone; Seeks ...anity Test.

1929 FLAPPERS EAT UP VAL

6

In 1929, he had members of a **rival** gang killed. The public called for him to pay.

CHICAGO DAILY NEWS

THURSDAY, FEBRUARY 14, 1929.—FORTY-EIGHT PAGES.   FINAL EDITION

BLUE STREAK

RE 7 OF MORAN GANG

SCENE OF LATEST GANGSTER OUTBREAK

KILLING SCENE TOO GRUESOME FOR ONLOOKERS

View of Carnage Proves a Strain on Their Nerves.

IS LIKE A SHAMBLES

VICTIMS ARE LINED AGAINST WALL; ONE VOLLEY KILLS ALL

Assassins Pose as Policemen; Flee in "S—

HISTORY CONNECTION

Capone was a crime boss from 1925 to 1931. He made money selling alcohol and running gambling houses. Both were illegal at the time.

DECIDE TO CUT COOK ADRIFT IN

War to Finish Russell's Plan

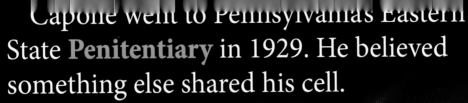

Capone went to Pennsylvania's Eastern State **Penitentiary** in 1929. He believed something else shared his cell.

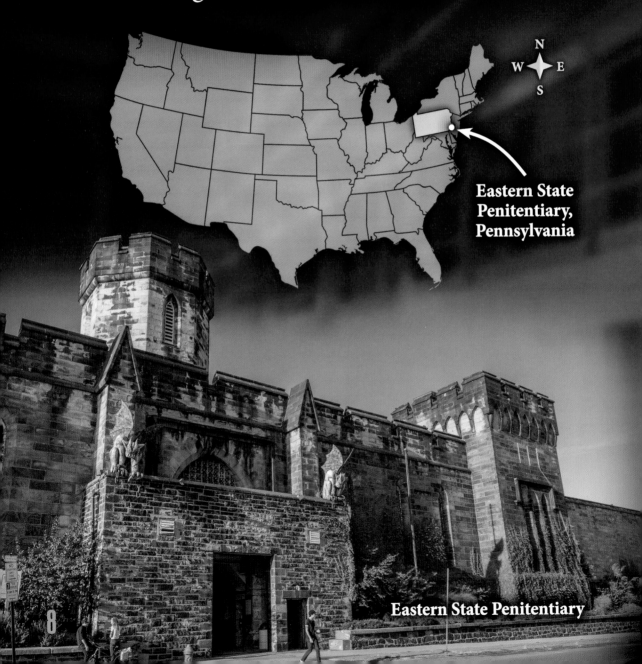

Eastern State Penitentiary, Pennsylvania

Eastern State Penitentiary

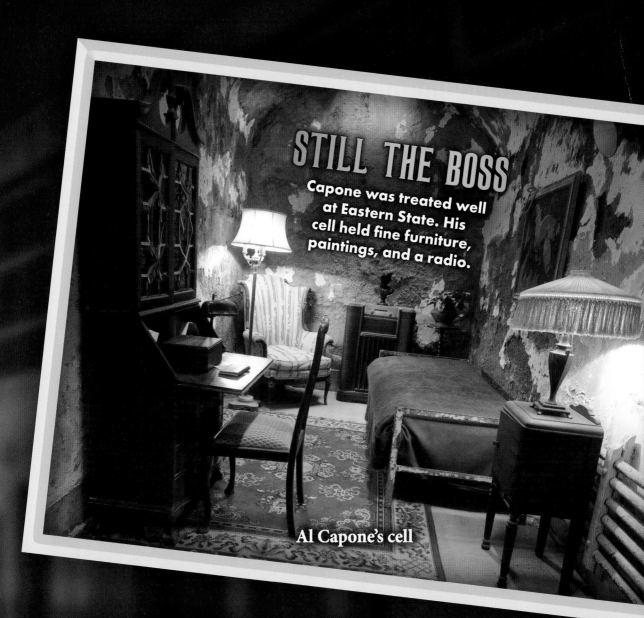

STILL THE BOSS

Capone was treated well at Eastern State. His cell held fine furniture, paintings, and a radio.

Al Capone's cell

Guards often heard him talking to "Jimmy." Capone would beg Jimmy to leave him alone.

James "Jimmy" Clark was killed by Capone's men. Perhaps his ghost came back to haunt the gangster.

Capone spent the next several years
in prison. He slowly lost his mind. Did
Jimmy's ghost push him toward madness?

SIGHTINGS AT EASTERN STATE PENITENTIARY

- Voices and evil laughter in Cellblock 12

- Ghostly shadows on walls in Cellblock 6

- Evil energy and ghostly figures from an opened cell

THE MAN WITH GLOWING EYES

Alcatraz stands on an island off California's coast. In the mid-1900s, it was a high-security prison.

EVIL ALCATRAZ

Native Americans avoided Alcatraz Island before the prison. They believed evil spirits lived there.

Inmates were treated poorly. Unlucky ones spent time in a tiny cell called the "Hole." They suffered in darkness and silence.

Alcatraz, California

N
W E
S

the Hole

screams echoed from the cell. He said he saw a man with glowing eyes. Guards thought he was either crazy or joking. They never checked on him.

HISTORY CONNECTION

Alcatraz was built to protect San Francisco Bay. Soon it became a prison. But it was expensive to keep up. Now it is open to the public.

The next morning, guards found the man dead. A look of horror was frozen on his face. Mysterious handprints marked his throat.

It seemed something
else *had* been in the cell.
And it had killed him!

SIGHTINGS AT ALCATRAZ

- Prisoner reappears after being strangled to death

- Visitor meets a spirit that looks like "Butcher," a prisoner who was murdered

- People hear banjo music coming from where Capone used to play

HAUNTINGS OR HALLUCINATIONS?

Some think **mental illness** caused Capone to see Jimmy's ghost.

Others believe the opposite. They say Jimmy's ghost and Alcatraz are what drove Capone **insane**.

BREAKING AL

Al Capone was in Alcatraz from 1934 to 1939. There, he had no special treatment. After five years, his mind was nearly gone.

The Alcatraz inmate also may have **hallucinated**. Many believed a guard **strangled** him. Yet other inmates claimed to see the man with glowing eyes, too.

Perhaps some prison **sentences** never end, even in death.

GLOSSARY

disturb—to bother or disrupt

gangster—a member of a group of dangerous criminals

hallucinated—saw or heard something that was not there

inmates—people locked in a prison

insane—unable to properly understand reality

mental illness—a condition that affects mood, thoughts, and behavior

penitentiary—a prison that holds criminals found guilty of serious crimes

rival—competing

sentences—punishments given by a court of law

strangled—killed by choking

TO LEARN MORE

AT THE LIBRARY

Gordon, Nick. *Alcatraz*. Minneapolis, Minn.: Bellwether Media, 2014.

Higgins, Nadia. *Ghosts*. Minneapolis, Minn.: Bellwether Media, 2014.

Williams, Dinah. *Haunted Prisons*. New York, N.Y.: Bearport Publishing, 2014.

ON THE WEB

Learning more about ghosts in prisions is as easy as 1, 2, 3.

1. Go to www.factsurfer.com.

2. Enter "ghosts in prisons" into the search box.

3. Click the "Surf" button and you will see a list of related web sites.

With factsurfer.com, finding more information

INDEX